In the Midnight Sky

Katacha Díaz
illustrated by Elizabeth Buttler

Captain Amy is a pilot.
She flies her plane late at night
high up in the sky
when everyone is fast asleep.

She flies her plane

over big cities and small towns
when everyone is fast asleep.

She flies over mountains and deserts

and over farmers' fields
when everyone is fast asleep.

She flies her plane over rivers and lakes

and over stormy oceans
when everyone is fast asleep.

Captain Amy flies her plane in the wind

and through the clouds
when everyone is fast asleep.

Her plane goes higher and faster

through the clouds and
leaves a trail of footprints in the sky.

Bright stars and the silvery moon

light the way
high up in the midnight sky.

Captain Amy loves
to fly her plane late at night
when everyone is fast asleep.